DARK MOON NEW MOON

DARK MOON NEW MOON

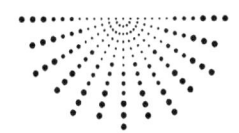

LUNA SERANOVA

CONTENTS

For Maddie & Megan,
who always answered the phone.

And to my dad,
the only man who never made me cry—you're kind of a big deal.

"The greatest thing you'll ever learn is just to love and be loved in return."

— Nat King Cole, "Nature Boy"

CONTENT WARNING

Some of the poems in this book deal with domestic violence and suicidal ideation, which some readers may find distressing. As always, take care of yourself, and reach out to a trusted mental health professional if you need help.

National Domestic Violence Hotline
    800-799-7233

National Suicide Hotline
    1-800-273-TALK (8255)
    or call/text 988

A NOTE FROM LUNA

Rarely have I ever sat down to write a poem.

Far more often than not, I wake to a poem on my lips, begging me to memorialize it on paper.

I believe in the concept that ideas are not your own, but rather cosmic nudges. As if your spirit guides are sending you a letter with a gift in it, and you can choose to use it— to take action, or not. But if you don't, know that someone else will. While it's true that I sat down and wrote the words onto paper as soon as they came to me, I view myself more as a channel for the creativity that my Muses gifted me.

These poems speak not just of my own experiences, but of the collective feminine. The wounded lover in each of us. The dreamer, too.

They say there are only seven stories. We're all just expanding on them in our own ways. I am honored to be among the poets, among the authors and creatives and visionaries who have put pen to paper and created beauty— even if just for a moment— in a world so dark. I am honored that you are here, I am beyond words that you have granted me a moment of time in your precious life to let me tell you a story.

Between these pages you'll find two parts: Dark Moon, and New Moon. The poems that lie within the Dark Moon section were written during endings, heartbreak, and extremely low moments in my life. The dark moon represents not only the darkest moment in the lunar cycle, but also the most vulnerable, raw, and real that you can get. A time of pure shadow realization and recognition, if you're willing to face it. I am no stranger to the dark moon. While intense and underworldly, it is an honor to explore the depth of human emotion and existence— albeit often difficult. It is truly always darkest before the dawn, and I believe you will see that reflected in these poems.

The New Moon section holds poems of regrowth, hope, beauty, and love. The dark moon is needed to shed all that holds us back— like the Tower card in the Tarot, paving the way for us to create a new, better existence. If the dark moon is the Tower, the new moon is the Star card. The New Moon poems are hope fossilized. The remembrance of beauty and color and love— most importantly, self-love.

We each will go through dark and new moon phases over and over in our lives. I hope that you feel seen in all your darkness within the Dark Moon pages, and that you remember to dream and hope within the New Moon.

I hope that you remember the beauty and the joy always.

xoxo,
Luna

PART ONE
DARK MOON

LORE OF A LOVER

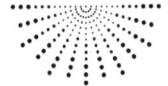

My desire to be loved
despite everything
was my gift
and a curse.

PSYCHOPOMP DREAMING OF SUN

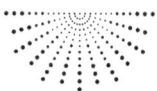

Daughter of liminal spaces; the in-betweens

Autumn and Spring
enamored by extremes,
love and dreams

Reaching and reaching
for some new beginning

My purpose is dreaming
my religion is longing
it seems I'm stuck
in the machine.

SAVIOR

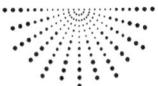

A chirp sounds at the foot of my bed
and a shadow of fur with pointed ears
hurls its body toward me—

reading my thoughts

restraining my hands
with all its weight
four paws on hands wet with tears
as it lays its body upon my chest
vibrating life back into my heart

and I think
at least for now
I'll stay.

TWENTY-FIVE

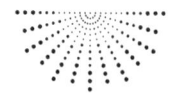

For my birthday this year
I made a cake
had invited some new friends

I sat under the park gazebo
in a salt circle of canvases
and watercolor paints
enough for eight

But the cake stared mockingly back at me
with its cherry accessory
and elaborate makeup

An hour passed I spent waiting
for only the rain to arrive
and wash away
the color from my painting.

TO FALL IN LOVE UNDER THE
GOLDEN SUN

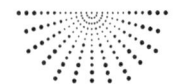

I fell in love with the California sun
like you fall in love at sixteen;
eager, romanticized
blinded by his radiance

California,
sweet like honey
mean but beautiful
tied up like Shibari
I gave my body

I thought it'd be different
but that's the thing
when you're in love like sixteen
you really think
you can change him

and I really thought
I could change the city.

SLEEPING IN P. BEACH

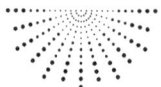

Can I leave a part of me in California?

Leave a fraction of my soul
fossilized
deep within the sands of Pacific Beach
staring up at the misty morning
letting the sun beams paint me golden
through the cracks of the boardwalk above
like the state I love?

Because I just want to hear the sea gulls

and remember.

IT DOESN'T HAPPEN TO WOMEN
I KNOW

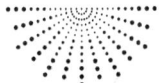

"It doesn't happen to women I know"

But I can tell you the story
of when I said no

I was seventeen
he was twenty

and no to him

meant ask me again
and again
and again
and again

until I cried

because what was I
if I wasn't pleasing my guy?

And then he had to show his brother
the photos I took

when I was young and sweet and sixteen

he had to; he said
his brother made him

but what say did I get?

My naive body something to show,
something to own

like a prized fish you caught
to show off

but that was my fault, they'll say
I should have known how men think

And it's not just me

it's not unique

it's her story
and her story
and her story

for all of history.

EVERGREEN

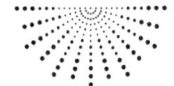

Malignant memories
stay like the constant scent of evergreen
their dirty hue etched into my mind
a stain on my faded jeans
something small
every day
to remind me.

INNOCENCE OF EIGHTEEN

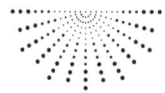

Mirror, Mirror, on the wall

Who is the sanest of us all?
Mirrors, Mirrors, suppress my calls
my mind, some sadist, loves to recall—
never have I seen such mirrors so unclear
these footsteps I recognize
now grow nearer and nearer
his laser eyes blaze through my soul—
this hasn't happened in years—
his shove hurls me into some vortex
where I'm in the old two story, like before,
where those I love can't see
what's happening,
like before

but it doesn't end the same.

BORN TO LOVE /
FORCED TO FIGHT

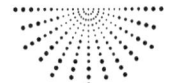

I have never loved a man
who didn't grow to hate me.

One who didn't raise their voice,
throw things,
and sheepishly apologize
beg
like a dog scorned.

And I wonder what in me
causes such fear in them?
Such a need to riot,
a disdain for peace?

What silently stirs in me?
And what does it awake
in men?

I'M JUST A GIRL!
(IN A MAN'S WORLD)

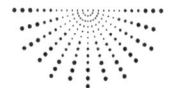

I am tired
of begging the men in my life to go to therapy
and paying the price for their sins
when they don't.

AMERICA IS THE POOREST NATION ON EARTH

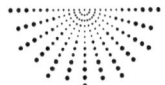

Emotional intelligence has no currency
when trading romances with a man.

BLACK HOLE / DEEP SEA / DO YOU STILL LOVE ME?

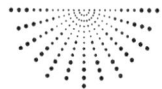

I can't imagine a man
who would love me wholly.

Someone who didn't mind the sadness
and loved to tell me how much he loved me.

A man who could look
into the eye of the black hole that is my heart—
the deep seas of my mind
and sort through the depth
and kiss me as I wept
and not turn around the next day
to tell me I'm too sensitive.

PSYCHIC V PSYCHOSIS

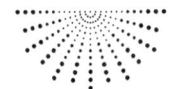

There are things
I want to talk about
but you just get mad
too defensive to hear me out

So I lay in bed
telling the ghost in the corner of my room
and crying to the voices in my head
because they listen

and I pretend they're you.

DAUGHTER OF LILITH

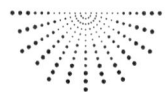

My heart is a poison—
my kiss a curse
infecting men from the inside out

Love so deep it burns
through the skin
revealing their heart

and that's the worst fate

because a vulnerable man
will soon be angry

and filled with hate.

A BARGAIN WITH A RUTHLESS GOD

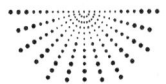

If you want to leave me,
do it.

You're edging me
with a knife at my throat

You're dancing around
putting on a performance
but I don't care

I just want the truth

And if you're going to leave me,
do it
while I'm young

spare me my youth
spare me my time.

VENUS RETROGRADE

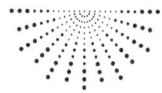

Damiana, honey, and rose petals
dress my cherry wood altar

Amber liquid drips down my fingers—
my hands falter

I reach for the pink candle
laid gently near the herbs

but it's too late.

I don't think Venus wants to save us.

POMEGRANATE

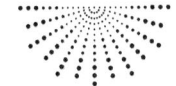

My soul used to write poems
of love and beauty
sing of color and life
and spring and summer
and wind and waves

I long for that life in me again

I long to feel the breeze
the July sun and the afternoon sea

I hope I am simply serving my six months
in my underworld

So I seduce the darkness
one pomegranate at a time

Spring on my lips
hope in my mind.

POISONED / PRISONER

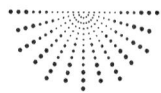

I lost
in the only war that mattered—
in the conquest of love

I was captured
stripped bare
gave myself so easily
and it ruined me

Poisoned me from the inside out
charcoal to the touch

My once pink and ripe body
now crumbles apart
in my lover's hands.

LILITH UNDER THE MASK OF EVE

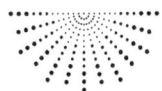

I ask you not to hurt me
so I don't have to remember

don't have to feel that
vampiric demon
within
taking over
hungry for blood
and ready to kill

We don't come
from the same rib
you couldn't imagine
where I've been

If you love me
please—
don't invite in
my sin.

BANSHEE IN THE NIGHT

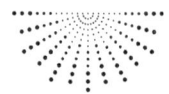

The easiest way
to meet the devil
is not to have sinned and die

but to hurt me

To lie to my face—
to deceive me

It's not pretty
it's not even right
certainly not love and fucking light

No,

My pain is a banshee in the night
my heart burns so hot—
words chill to the core
something you abhor

So don't act surprised

when the love of your life
turns out to be
a demon at your door.

MEDUSA

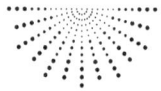

I had never screamed at someone
until a man screamed at me

Never was violent
until a man taught me

Now my throat is bleeding
and I'm a monster.

ARIES STELLIUM //
BROKEN HEART

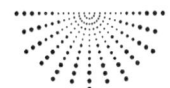

I want to write a letter of hate.

I want to spill out the hot molten anger
from my core
and stain the pages with the black ink
pulsing through my heart
which once beat softly for you

but as I do
I lose my fucking mind.

Weeping eyes wipe away the words on the page
and sizzle out the fire,
the last thing left of me,
until I'm filled with nothing at all
and address the letter of hate

to myself.

BEAUTIFUL, PAINFUL MUSE

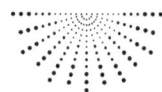

When we first met
I thought I'd never be able to write
a sad poem again.

Now,
I have an anthology full of them.

HEARTBREAK
[ALT TITLE: I THOUGHT YOU'D NEVER HURT ME]

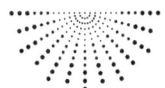

Heartbreak is walking through
a barren forest

Your favorite lush garden
burnt to ashes
black snow on the ground

The oak tree's shade
that covered the sun's burning rage
the little creatures and their homes
all of a sudden-
gone.

TO LOVE

is to welcome the dagger through your heart
and thank it
upon its withdrawal.

LOVE, LOSS, AND THE FORCE

There was a video—
two distressed women
one with grief, the other with fear

A mother dying
by the disease of forgetting
And a daughter trying

I cried
as I imagined my own mother

How cruel
the force of existence is

to make people suffer
and make others watch.

PISCES MOON

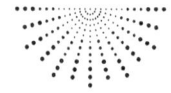

I feel debilitated
by the fragility of existence

the unbearable pain of grief
this unending and immense sentience;
merciless and omnipresent
and horribly aware

No escape from the influence of the heart.

PRETTY GIRL, SILLY GIRL

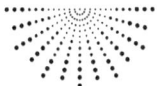

I am not the type of girl you look at
and think—

She's a sad girl

She's a girl who has toyed with the idea of death
in a many different ways,
settling almost romantically
on the blade

intimate and involved as it is.

Only choosing that monogamous love
after balancing the practicality of the gun,
but deciding it was too easy,
too separate

Weighing the pros and cons of each medium
of death—

Which would give the most room
to second guess?

Which could leave the least mess?

No one thought to worry about me.

No,
I am the girl you look at and think—

How pretty!
How vapid!
Bubbly and silly, always laughing.
No clue of reality.

No clue of reality.

PEARL

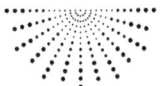

All the pretty pills
I take to keep me functioning
they're pearls around the neck
adorning who I used to be

like beads around Marilyn
she wore them as she fell asleep

Maybe we should have fed
our jewelry to the sea.

UNTIL TOMORROW

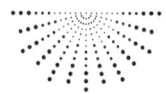

I can't die tonight—
my friends will be on FaceTime soon

And next week's no good
It's my niece's fifth birthday party
and grandma would be sad

No time in the next ten years—
I don't want my nephew
looking out at his graduation
wondering why auntie didn't show

and after that?

Well,
I'm sure there'll be another sunrise

Another cat on my lap
that would wait for me to come home

So I raise the blade
and cut my hair instead.

Promising myself another day

until the birds stop singing
until the moon stops shining.

PSYCHOSIS V PSYCHIC

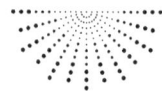

A fundamental part of me is missing
there is something wrong

My poetry has become darker and darker
like an ink death omen
dripping down the pages of me

and I'm scared of the growing darkness.

LIFE IN NOIR

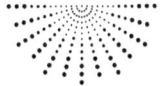

"Look," I say
The empty house looks back
"I made a painting of us—"
The canvas is dripping black

CRYPTID OF THE NIGHT IN A NIGHTGOWN

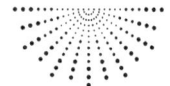

Darkness has overtaken me
shadow seeps through my veins
hard hollow heart
weighted corpse
cursed mind

VOID

I can't even write
but I'm no longer sad
I truly feel
nothing at all

APATHY: A JOURNAL ENTRY

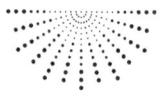

I haven't written a poem in weeks. My writings generally stem from the insufferable symptom of being a Pisces moon.

Recently there's been a gaping hole replacing what used to be a seismic pulsating of sadness. Like the middle of the ocean; dark and vast and empty and cruel. Quiet. And void of...anything. Void of art. Void of feeling.

Void of meaning.

So I lay in bed. Paralyzed by the impending change of...life —of everything. Seeing my future steam rolling toward me like a semi-truck. And I'm a butterfly in the road with its wings cut. I can do nothing but watch. Watch this version of me take her last breaths and see her/my spirit evaporate with each dying breath.

I think maybe everything will be okay despite it all.

I think I'll write again, and I think I'll sing. I think I'll laugh and eat good food and feel romantic.

Romance is like oxygen to me, and I've been drowning.

PART TWO
NEW MOON

SEVENTEEN

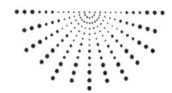

I will never be a girl again.

Never again be seventeen with a dream—
stupid and happy

Time won't stop moving
and I keep having to meet
all these new versions of me.

LITERARY PRIESTESS

Life is gray and cold
but when I'm between pages
the Gods grant me peek into this life
of color and romance and love and
warmth and meaning and feeling

and I get to forget
and I get to hope.

HEKATE

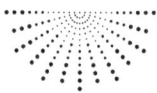

Hail Hekate!
We chanted in the bounds of our circle
our voices shook the walls
with Her holy epithets,
her presence like opium held in the air

As if taken by that prophetic herb,
a flash of remembrance
coursed through my psyche
and in between orphic hymns
the realization occurred:

This Sacred Chthonic Queen
had graced me with her spirit
some days before this holy night
when a stranger
a young mother
begged of me my truth.

I had never heard of her
but we shared one link

She spoke of this man,
whose name I had spent years trying to forget
And after she told her story
of cruel love
she asked me of mine

The trauma stuck in my throat and in my body

To whom do I owe my truth?

Must I retell the stories?
Feel once again the deathly taste of terror
on my lips at the memories?
Feel through the words his hands
holding me down?
His car racing through town to track me down?
And how far do I go?

How much does she need to know?

Can the currency of knowledge
pay her way out of this grave?

I heard that foreign sickening voice
beneath my thoughts,
implanted by the Jupiterian-ruled
man himself:

Must I commit the unspeakable crime
of using my voice against a man?

Must I speak the truth which demands justice?

For years I was silenced

Convinced I could buy my peace

with pacification—
because just a single word would warrant a threat
from the man who took my youth

But by the grace of the Great Mother,
I spoke

I held nothing back

In tearing open these wounds
I thought I'd bleed out

What I didn't realize
until this ritual
was that I gave this young woman
what no one gave me

And by the will of Hekate,
We were both free.

MONSIEUR CHAT

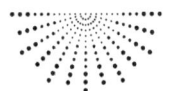

Parisian cat in the window
looking down at me
I wonder what you know?

Our eyes watch each other
bridging Rue Montmartre
Do you love watching the people below?
Do their noises interest you?

Sitting in our open frames
cradled against the warm breath of the furnace
I wonder your name

You soft thing
with eyes like coal
and a coat like a flat white

I leave tomorrow
and after that
I won't be here each morning
to watch the people with you

But you appeared so quickly
that first Thursday I set my bags down
and released the sun from behind the blinds

I know you know more than me
that once I leave,
someone else will come
someone new to keep company.

DIRT BODY, SACRED GHOST

When I die,
pour out a sweet tea
and plant catnip at my grave

Let me become a tree
and place a bench under my shade
so you can read me
your favorite poetry

Tell me your troubles
and sing me a song

Leave a peony
on the earth for me
and don't leave me
for long.

RUE MONTMARTRE

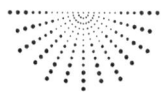

Looking out the open window
at the cobblestone streets below
the people go and the people go
and the people go

My damp hair slicks down the side of my neck
as I dry it
while across the way and a story out
sits a white cat, staring back
I blow him a kiss

A moment ago
I sliced open my toe
on the sharp raised entry of the bedroom

I didn't notice
until the cold blood dripped
down onto the vinyl wood floors

Tonight, I'll rest.
I'll be Paris' eyes

And still, I think I'm happier
than if I were those people
go go going.

6AM IN LA

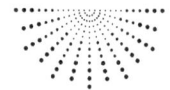

I did not incarnate to Earth
and taste the sweet grass
of the rolling hills
to work each second away
just to pay bills

Am I like the birds?
standing way up high
on their electric thrones-
perched posture; cackling
watching the worker ants of humanity
forget why they're here
as they rush and rush and rush

I think I am the house cat
Sitting on you-
begging
For you to take a break
and simply just be

Please, I'd purr—

sit with me
and watch the birds
watching the people.

I DREAM OF MAGIC

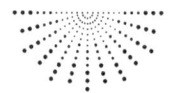

I don't dream of work

I dream of pleasure—
of sitting on the floor in my vine-lined home,
homemade pizza warming the hands
of the people who've known me
my whole life

I dream of resting—
of watching the wind flirt
with the autumn leaves
outside my window

I dream of magic
and seeing my loved ones fall in love

I dream of singing while doing the dishes
underscored by the sound of family laughing
in the room over.

LA DEVOTEE /
MARQUEE DETAINEE

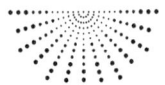

I still love you, LA
even with how you treated me

It's not your fault, really—
haunted by the ghosts
of people like me,
used by dreamers daily,
a romanticized reality
you didn't ask to be

But I loved you before I met you—

dreamt of you—

knew we were destined by soul ties;
my karmic dream,
and I'll always love you

Maybe we're meant to be
in another life
or another time

But I'll always be another girl
with your name tattooed
like neon lights.

WHY DO I STAY ALIVE?

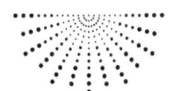

For the soft-hued pastel tinted clouds
spreading in the dusk sky like an artists' palette,
looking back at me; small and centered
eyes wide at the sky's beauty

For reading your new favorite book
for the first time,
kicking your little feet
and crying at ink on a page

The first sip of your iced coffee in the morning
and feeling alive under the summer sun

For licking icing off the candles
of your homemade birthday cake
surrounded by folks you love

For making love
again and again and again and again

and falling in love

For the warmth of the cat sitting on my lap
who acts disinterested and aloof
but who I know would lay on my bed waiting
for me to return.

PRAYER OF THE MAIDEN

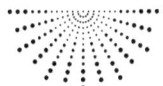

I will not wilt before I'm twenty-three

I will not pluck my beauty for a dream
of someone who may love or love me not

While I am that rose,
and that rose is me,
there are infinite more things I could be.

VENUS IN AQUARIUS

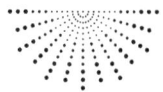

Daydreaming of how a lover
would write me:

"Contrasting the soft porcelain curve of her back,
her raven hair cascades,
leading like midnight river Styx
toward her soft hips
twilight eyes twinkle;
scorpionic deep seas
and tattoos that run up her ivory arms
like ivy
warm breath
pomegranate lips
like a divine siren lures me in."

And I wonder
how to get a lover
who would compose songs
about my laughter
someone who would know the cause
of each different roar
intimately

Someone who would write about
the shades of blue
in my eyes
and in my mind
and recognize the certain look of nostalgia
when it takes over me
A lover who honored the fierce red-hot passion
of my soul
and lightness of my desire

Who could paint by memory
the gray in my eyes before sunlight warms them
or the image of me in the morning
hair tousled with sleep

Someone who would know
how I fell in love
with the idea of love

and maybe instead of my body
they'd write of my mind

and maybe
be in love with both.

TWENTY- SIX

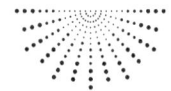

Today I'm twenty-six

and the morning sun is warm
on my skin

and it's spring again

Leo rises over the horizon
marking my fate this round—

and the clovers are loud with fragrance
dancing around the dandelions in the yard

and I think
I think I'll be okay.

GIRLHOOD

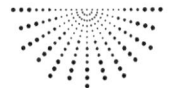

There is a vulnerability to girlhood
the Monistat unabashed dressing the nightstand

the towers of books with their rainbow of spines
in perfect order and chaos

and me

hunching close to the mirror
criss-cross on a fluffy pink heart-shaped rug
hair held back by an old silk scarf
half a set of false lashes

barely holding on

praying my affirmations
into the most expensive oil I own
and a rose quartz gua sha

"I am pretty"

"I am worthy"

"I am worthy"

A WOMAN FREE

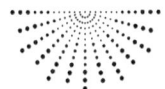

Though men have taught it for centuries,
your sexualization of me
is not my responsibility

Your attraction to me
holds no gravity
over my own autonomy

So sad—
That my body simply existing
could be so upsetting
so arousing—
so distracting—
to witness

So I'll wear a shorter skirt,
hair up so the curve of my collarbone
is on display
Post my after-shower mirror pics
to desensitize the wound
of witnessing a Woman Free.

G.W.B.B.

I rise with feminine power

My hips
an atrocity

My lips
raising anarchy

This body
a delicacy
belonging to me
and only me

Embodiment
my only philosophy

Empowerment
my legacy

Stand with me,
your majesty,

and reclaim
your destiny.

A CONFIDENT WOMAN

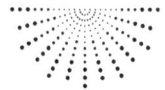

A confident woman is not born

She is not delivered into the world
knowing how to smile at her flaws
or how to say "no"

A confident woman is often
self-transmuted

Frankenstienianly puzzled together
from a girl who was both too much
and not enough

I have never met a confident woman
who knew her worth as a young girl
saw her own face in her mother as she
smiled at her cellulite and lines

The women I know have been through the
fire and flames and pulled their charred
souls out of the hands of the world
who told them

to fix everything

The most confident women I know
have felt the depths of self-hatred
heard their mother's self-hatred
were praised for how skinny they are
and reminded to
"Be thankful"
for that golden trophy is ephemeral

The most confident women I know
were told to lighten up
calm down

"It was just a joke!"

The most confident women I know
were not born confident
but rather birthed themselves
through a gauntlet of redefining
Womanhood

The most confident women I know
hope to be the first generation
that births confident women.

WITCH // WOMAN

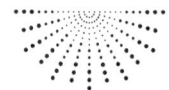

To be a girl is to be perceived by all
but truly known by few

To be lusted after, gawked at
But take it as a compliment, too

Because that means your pretty—
the best thing you can be

Pretty and nice
and good and clean

To be a witch is to reject it all
and know yourself true

To be wild and matted
and own your body, too

Because that means you're in control
the best thing you can be

Feral and wise;
Autonomous Queen.

GODDESS OF LOVE: YOU, TOO

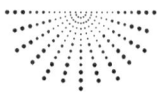

and you didn't realize,
as you filled your home
with roses and candles
and offerings to the Goddess,
that simply by honoring
the Divine Feminine
you fell back in love with yourself

by honoring the Goddess,
you healed yourself

the roses, for your Goddess,
made your home a beautiful sanctuary

the chocolate offering
(which you also had a piece of)

the glamour magic,
gave you the power to control
how you were perceived

And by honoring the Goddess of Love,
you fell back in love
with love
and with life.

SOLAR PROTECTOR

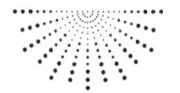

This morning I was awoken by a rush
of warm morning sunshine to my left

Suddenly I was no longer suffering
from the loneliness
of the nightmare before

The Sun knows,
and wraps me in his protection

I am safe once more.

TAURUS RISING

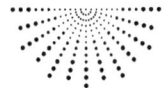

I can't help but feel romantic
about existing.

ECLIPSE

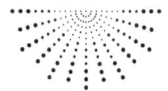

If the eclipse
is the end of the world
then I'll eat an entire pizza
and be glad that I had a campfire last night
surrounded by family
and ran through the grass
of my childhood home

I'll spend the day
writing a novel I'll never finish
forgetting about taxes and emails

I'll eat cake, too
and kiss the cats
I'll plant a garden
and water the rose bush once more

And when hell opens
and the world floods
I'll be away
dreaming
of love.

LOVE DEVOTEE

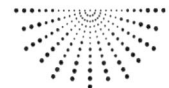

Freckles on your faces
like stars in a constellation—
I pray to the astrology of you

Write me a horoscope and I'll
do as you want me to

Tell me—
when is an auspicious time
to love you?
To drink in your body like sacred wine
at the altar of your heart?

I'll worship you, my love,
blood sacrifice
take my body's vitality

I'd drain myself
as a formality.

SILK SHEETS AND YOU

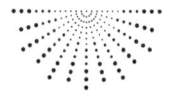

In your presence
I feel like a mortal woman
making love to a God

Underneath silk sheets I'm a priestess
praying to you breathlessly

Your sheer strength
through warm and calloused
and gentle hands
pinning me to the bed
reminding me my own frailty
under a glimmer of your power

A loving deity

That's why I love being on my knees for you

My lips, a means of devotion—
worshiping, tasting,
drinking in the holy sacrament of your body.

THE ROMANTIC'S CURSE

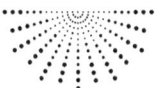

You can scream it to the stars—
whisper into the notches of the willow tree

You can write it down
with a lip-stained seal
smearing the sweet taste
like the pink ink down the page

You can pray to your goddess
or ask Eros for his blessing

But no matter what you do
you can't stop it
from consuming you.

ECSTASY

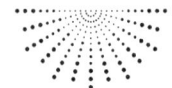

I want to impale myself on him—
solid deep into my core,
gasping for breath
begging for more

Give me that petite death

I want to feel his sweet honey
dripping warm
down my chest
in between
fingertips

I want to drown in the taste
savor the chase
the ecstasy of men
and when it's over

Do it again
Do it again
Do it again.

PLASTIC CUP OF SAZERAC

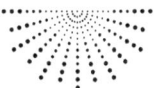

Cloud like smoke climbed the heights
of our bisque kitchen walls
dim like the back room of a speakeasy
kissed with the scent of wildflowers foraged

and we danced, and we danced,
to the beat of the beeps

bare feet on linoleum
seemingly floating into those
kitchen clouds

Until we settled down
criss-cross on the ground

We'll watch whatever he wants
I'll kiss him on the cheek
and we'll finish the night eating
whatever it was we burnt again
cold drink in hand.

ONCE YOU FALL IN LOVE
WITH ME

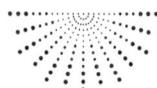

I'm limitless

The kind of woman
Hozier sings about
dreams about

Walking through the midnight woods
bare feet over mossy ground
praying to the stars out loud
scream into the void about
the way my lips taste after dark
cherry sin down your neck
through your heart
the coolness of my eyes gray and sharp
blue and green and mean

no turning back
no turning back

once you fall in love with me.

CAN I CALL YOU ROSE?

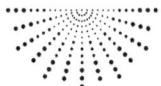

Let me watch you blossom

Your eager red petals reach up
into the fresh winds of new life

Your bright leaves still wet
with the dew of youth
and curiosity,

You don't hesitate

No,
you haven't learned
to fear the unknown yet

They'll call you "ignorant"
Stay ignorant

Only those who still believe
in the strength of their own roots

Will have the courage to bloom and exist
in their essential land.

RIBBONS AND ICING AND ROSES

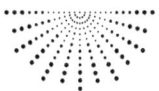

I hope someday you realize
life can be gentle

life can be easy and fun and soft
and you don't always have to be so careful
don't have to raise your voice to be listened to
always expecting the worse

Life can be ribbons and icing and roses

you can have your cake and eat it
and make another one tomorrow

and you don't have to be so scared
of feeling it all.

NYX

I hope that even in all my darkness,
I was beautiful.

ACKNOWLEDGMENTS

Self-publishing is a feat in itself, but never done alone, and I owe an incredible thank you to all the talented creatives who made this possible. Thank you to Mitch Green for the cover design, it's as hauntingly beautiful as my soul and for that I'm ever grateful. Thank you to Robert Harrison from Seneca Author Services for helping me to make a beautiful book out of these thoughts! Thank you to Stephanie Kemler for always supporting me and letting me blow up your phone with question after question as I enter this crazy world of writing. Thank you to Tyson for not letting me fall into an existential artist's crisis while editing.

Thank you to my parents, who never told me a dream was too big or too crazy. I know my artistic and creative abilities were nurtured well from day one. Thank you to Grandma, for giving me the author gene. Thank you to Zach for it all, the dark and the light, every day is a gift with you, and I love you. Thank you to my friends, Maddie, Megan, Kat, Kristian, Abi- you are all the light of my life and I love you with my whole heart (can we live in the same city again, please?)

Thank you to the Divine Feminine, the Goddess, for flowing through me in so many of these poems. Every day is a dedication to the divine. Thank you to my deities, my spirit guides, my muses, and my ancestors.

And finally, I would never forget to thank my Moon Fam. Thank you to every subscriber, every follower, every patron, every supporter. You have often been the brightest part of my day. I always dreamed of being a YouTuber, and because of your support, I really am. I will never be able to express my gratitude for you in words, but I hope for now this suffices. I love you all so much!

Thank you reader, for joining me in the space, and bearing witness to the dark and the light. In your darkest of dark moons, may you always remember the new moon.

xoxo,
Luna

ABOUT THE AUTHOR

 Luna Seranova is an author, glamour witch, and Freyja devotee with a mission to demystify the taboo. Filling her days with magic, mysticism, and cats, she shares her adventures on YouTube with over 30k subscribers. Between tarot and astrology readings, she spends her days writing and dreaming. Dark Moon New Moon is her debut book.

Find Luna at @LunaSeranova, or LunaSeranova.com

www.ingramcontent.com/pod-product-compliance
Lightning Source LLC
Chambersburg PA
CBHW060332130626
46553CB00003B/984

* 9 7 9 8 2 1 8 4 3 3 3 4 5 *